A PAROCHIAL VIEW
OF GLASGOW

By
ALFRED FORBES SMITH

First published in Scotland
in 1997
by
A.A. Enterprises.

Typeset by Edward M. Skelly, Berwick upon Tweed.
Printed by Martins the Printers, Spittal, Berwick upon Tweed.

ACKNOWLEDGEMENTS

To The Mitchell Library in Glasgow for their help, and reproduction of photographs shown in this book.

To "The Daily Record" for providing original photographs of Benny Lynch.

To Yarrow Shipbuilders Ltd for copy of Princess Alexandra at the launching of H.M.S. Broadsword, 12th May 1976.

FOREWORD

A nostalgic view of Glasgow, as seen through the eyes of a man who has observed it well. A strong visual imagery through words, showing Glasgow and her people in days long gone, never to return.

Thousands of Glaswegians will be able to relate to the work contained in this book and perhaps reminisce a little too.

Assunta Arrighi
Editor

"If you forget where you came from, then you'll never know where you are going."

Alfred Forbes Smith, born and bred in The Garngad, Glasgow.
Worked as a welder in John Brown's Shipyard in Clydebank. It was here he found so much material for his writing career.
Retired in 1990 due to industrial injuries – a legacy of the Shipyards.
Began writing extensively, reflecting on his journey through life in his beloved home town of Glasgow.

Photograph taken by John O'Malley.

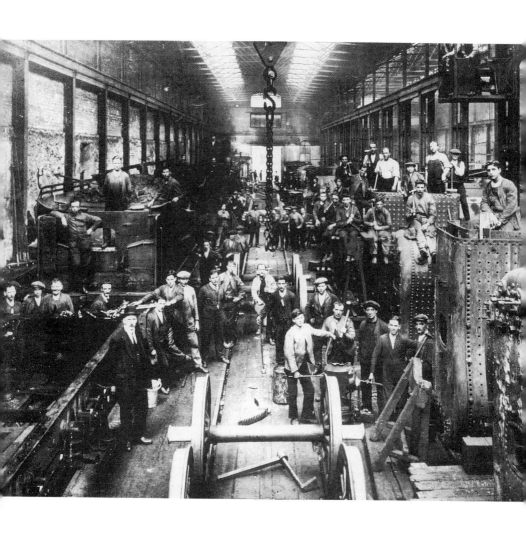

Photo: Courtesy of The Mitchell Library, Glasgow.

SHIPYARDS

Cauld, dank gloomy places that naebody ran tae readily,
except hand in hand wi' expediency, and well-worn habit.
Haunting sheds, where ghosts of yesterday's scenario still wander
'midst plates and nerves of steel,
custodians of a history steeped in blood,
...tae price a meal.

In craft, you spawned better men unconsciously,
than sober, would-be nobler, places could,
where phoney pitiful pretence,
was naewhere tae be found,
'mongst honest graft.

A place, where culinary skills abounded,
as 'pieces' in sausages and eggs, beetroot, and black puddin',
spam, jam, Belfast ham, mince an' tatties, and mutton,
realised their full potential ower a Blacksmith's fire,
while a thousand personalised tea cans brewed in harmony,
tae the music o' a blast furnace,
...what aroma filled the air.

Monumental acres of consecrated soil,
beside Midwife rivers, wi' cobbled streets on nodding terms wi' Royalty,
where men and boys matured their dignity in daily toil,
...while rats looked on.

Rough security, tho' infinitely better than Social,
where Faith, Hope, and Survival,
and a slut called Denial,
copulated openly, to produce minds,
...ye couldnae pawn.

The proud, the humble, the know-all, the thing,
the forsakit, the glaikit, the eegit, the King,
the critic, the mystic, the bigot, the Knave,
the ambitious, the vicious, the coward,
...the BRAVE!

Hull 534 "The Queen Mary", built at John Brown's Shipyard, Clydebank 1934. Photograph: Courtesy of The Mitchell Library, Glasgow.

WHEN WE BUILT THE BIG SHIPS

'Twas a Monday morn and the snaw was blawin'
o'er Yarrows Yard in Scotstoun
when the lads did a dance thro' the big steel doors
in satorial elegance wi' their woolly drawers
and umpteen pair o' socks on.

The weekend that had passed
got a verbal blast
that was high up on the agenda
Celts and Rangers both had won
and the Pubs had made a ton
noo the money was a' done
"Pss, Hey Jimmy, hiv ye seen the money lender?"

Then slow but sure came a familiar noise
as the steel breathed life, in rythm wi' the boys
bolts were screwed and timber hewed
and engines put in position
gun turrets were marked
and welding rods sparked
"Naw...this boat's no' for fishin'!"

The giant cranes towered o'er the bleak shipyard
like massive grey flamingoes
letting oot their tongues, looking for food
as doon the oily sling goes
lifting loads here
an' laying them doon there
withoot even perspirin'
nae aches or pains
nae airms that were sair
for their diet wis strictly...iron.

And the cauld river blaws
excited the pace
of oor frozen fish-fingers
and blue tinted face
but oor bodies were conditioned
to beat the Big Freeze
by a can o' hot tea
an' a big 'piece' in cheese
and Dumbarton Road has premises
tae gie us some mair cheer
a wee bet in the Bookies
or a big pint o' beer.

Then in the afternoon we gave an encore
of oor efforts on the morn
workin' haun in haun taegether
for in spite o' the cauld weather
the Shipbuilding still goes on
for we're used tae this work
amongst damp an' cauld an' dirt
sometimes wi' heartbreak and pain
but we're all right Jack
the boilersuit's on oor back
but we've nae boilersuits on oor brain.

Ye see there's some high-up folks
that think that us blokes
represent the subservient knee
but they're never considerin'
that the goods we're deliverin'
sign freedom and seal dignity
as three thousand men
dae daily attend
tae the ship's every need
stage by stage
leavin' beds that are warm
for great deeds tae perform
fulfilling their Heritage.

Then the clock shouts "half fowr"
and the day's work is o'er
it's hame tae a big warm meal
for we've done oor wee bit
in the name o' This Land
tae satisfy the conscience
tae justify the man
and contentment's what we feel
and we started this morn
in cauld December's haun
when the snaw was blawin'
o'er Yarrows Yard in Scotstoun.

HMS BROADSWORD

The first Type 22 Frigate
designed and built by
Yarrow (Shipbuilders) Ltd

LAUNCHED 12th MAY 1976 by
HRH PRINCESS ALEXANDRA

Photograph: Courtesy of Yarrow (Shipbuilders) Ltd.

THE LADY

"People say I'm beautiful
and look at me in wonder
I'm well shaped
and well draped
magnificent in Splendour.

A Princess in our Sovereign's name,
shall say to me "God Bless"
while much beribboned Gentlemen,
I'll certainly impress.

Bands will play
in great array
and champagne will flow
but here is a story
that I want the world to know.

Everything that I am
from start to finish
is the handywork of men
a skill that won't diminish.

There's Wullie frae Brigton
and Sammy frae Govan
Tommy fae Tollcross
there Joe and Dick
and Pat an' Mick,
an' Calum fae Wester-Ross.

Different faces
different creeds
different ways of living
but they have a common bond,
when to the world they're giving
all the greatness that I am
all my power which is not sham.

Theirs is the wealth of this land
the skill they have in a humble hand
so when people wave at me
and as the applause thunders
my heart's with them
those mighty men.

You see
I am a brand new ship
to sail the seas with pride
and I'm salutin'
not the high falutin'
but My Sons...
The Shipbuilders of the Clyde!"

"The Innermost thoughts of H.M.S. Broadsword"

Launched 12th May 1976 by Princess Alexander.

AULD GLESGA TOON

Welcome tae the Toon o' Culture
Welcome tae the Land o' Youth
wi' millions coming o'er the watter
searching oor Eternal Truth

They'll clap oor backs
and sing oor praises
extol oor virtues
drink oor cheers

But we'll just shake
oor heids in wonder
the Keelies here
have known it a' for years.

Glasgow City of Culture 1990

Back Courts between Bright Street and Cobden Street. Courtesy of The Mitchell Library, Glasgow.

16

POVERTY

Poverty is about having no dreams...when all you do is dream,
about always making excuses...when you haven't done anything wrong.
It's about crying a lot...even when you're not peeling onions.
It's about always signing your autograph for the Provy Cheque Man.
It's about sometimes selling things...that shouldn't have price tags.
Or turning wine bottles into medicine bottles...because you're dancing on
broken bottles,
or asking the Butcher for bones for the dog...then inviting the dog
to dinner.
Or becoming an expert without any training...at hairdressing,
dressmaking, peacemaking, and economy.
Poverty is about doing your best...and always fearing the worse,
or seeking guidance...from three blind mice.
Or planning your future...with the Four Horsemen of The Apocalypse.
It's about knowing your own direction...but walking in somebody
else's shoes.
It's about accepting the unacceptable...because the choice is
always Hobsons.
Like living in an open prison...with Spiritual shackles and mental chains.
About saying prayers when Heaven is closed,
and cursing when Hell is open.
Is about being too sick to be ill...too afraid of what can scare,
too fed up to be sad...and too bothered to care.
Some people even think that Poverty is logical.
The poor live in Sociological Squalor...and die in Psychological Misery.
In conclusion Poverty is like bad language, and bad breath,
although we accept
these things as part of life...they can still be corrected.

If only man to man the world o'er lived by this simple maxim...
"Charity begins at home, but Justice begins next door"
Or is that too much to dream?

The Barras

THE BARRAS

Doon at the Barras, the music plays,
it's a good place, tae buy second haun claes.
It's the biggest store in Glesga Toon,
the revolving door, goes roon and roon.

People come and people go,
in the sun and in the snow,
if things look auld, when a bargain you seek,
then a bargain you'll get, "It's a real antique"

You'll get a quids worth for hauf a croon,
and the jokes are free when you're feeling doon
there's wulks and mussels, an' candy floss,
and Paddy the Strong Man, that lifts a horse.

Designer labels fae Gucci tae Armani,
but, "bought at the Barras," is good enough fur Granny,
you can write anything on your shopping list,
if you cannae get it here, then it disnae exist.

An Aladdin's Cave as exclusive as Harrods,
but a bit mair stylish, is the famous Glesga Barras,
the world o'er it hisnae an equal,
second haun claes, for first class people!

BLOOMIN' MAGIC

Every other house,
in every Street and Road,
had their ain Botanic Garden,
that wi' flowers overflowed,
and the vandals couldnae get tae it,
'though it had nae doors or locks,
'cause it was a great invention,
called a Glesga Windae Box!

"BUDDY, CAN YOU SPARE SOME TIME?"

Everyman has a story,
just as you have yours,
nae creature is sae lowly,
that ye canny lend yer ears.

So if a poor wee cowerin' man,
begs ye tae hear his plight,
listen in the morn,
because it might be yours the night!

THE JIGGIN

Oh for the days when Glesga wis swingin',
when big bands were playin' and live singers singin',
guys in drape suits and lassies in riggin',
a' dickied up furra night at the jiggin'.

The Barrowland...gaun yersel,
wi' Billy McGregor and Lena Martell,
the Locarno near tae Charing Cross,
hid Oscar Rabin and wee Joe Loss.

Ballroom lovers went to the Plaza,
wi' a fountain on the floor...what a Dazza,
Green's Playhouse hid Doctor Crock,
the Lindela Club had the Lindy Hop,
the magic Majestic wis a dancer's treat,
wi' stars in yer eyes and a twinkle in yer feet.

The Albert, the Astoria, an' the West End too,
were Fred Astaire's options...when he'd hid a few!
the F & F Ballroom doon Partick way,
wis a regular hotspot, for boogyin' the night away,
while the Palais-De-Danse in Dennistoon,
was the Lord O' The Dance goin' roon an' roon.

A million lumbars, a million marriages,
a million memories, a few wee disparages,
when wee Jeannie McColl became Mrs McGuigan,
and it a' began,
wi' a night at the Jiggin'!

THE SPARRA HAS LANDED

A wee Glesga sparra was crying in the rain,
so I took it up the stair 'cause I couldnae stand the pain,
and I laid it by the fire, like a drookit wee wean,
gied it some breid and milk and left it on its ain.

A few hours later I took a wee peek,
but the poor thing was deid, 'cause his beak dinnae tweek,
so I wrapped his remains in Hovis breid paper,
and put them in a margarine box, like a proper Undertaker.

Then the home-help took him doon, and laid him in the midden,
amongst a' the other wares, that had finished wi' life's biddin',
and the Doo's formed a Guard-of-Honour as a token o' affection,
waiting for the gun carriage, and the Funeral Procession.

Then on Monday morning along they came,
wi' the brash, pomp and ceremony, of All The King's Men,
uniformed in buttons of two's
as smart as any Guard,
were the Grenadiers in dirty shoes,
from St. Rollox Cleansing Yard.

And I cried a wee tear as I watched fae the windae,
'cause it's no' a sight ye often see,
on a dreich September Monday,
gettin' hurled oot in dignity in a midden man's barra,
was no' a bad send aff, for a wee Glesga Sparra!

Courtesy of The Mitchell Library, Glasgow.

24

THE PAWN

Of a' the riches in the world, the diamonds, jewels and gold,
there wis nane to compare,
with the treasure there,
held on loan in the Bright Street Pawn.

Herring-bone suits for twelve-and-a-tanner,
weddings rings still pledged wi' honour,
boots and shoes, and wally dugs,
tartan trews and Toby jugs.

Well used fiddles and penny-whistles,
frying pans and copper kettles,
pictures of Kilties surrounded wi' thistles,
in belts wi' buckles and bonnets wi' hackles.

Brass snuff boxes,
and stoles fae foxes,
openers for corks,
and bone-handled forks.

The Grandfather Clock had company on the wall,
for hauf o' the Garngads were hinging there as well,
and we telt the time by the Caley Bell,
in the timeless zone, roon the Bright Street Pawn.

But the greatest day in the Pawnbroker's life,
wis when somebody died, or took a wife,
then coats and suits, an' boots and shoes,
a' left the Pawn...for the Church's pews.

But on Monday morning, back they came,
a bit mair worn wi' the odd beer stain,
but he overlooked the wrangs did Uncle John,
t'was the Centre of Commerce..The Bright Street Pawn!

WHO AM I?

Every day
folks look for me
yet I am all around
for them to see.

I am a very important
commodity
to some I'm precious
to others free.

I'm North and South
and East and West
I'm Summer and Winter
and Autumn and Spring.

In memory
to some I'm best
to others
only sorrow bring.

Events would disrupt
if I stayed away
all mixed up
in disarray
but when I'm there
they smoothly run
I'm good, I'm bad
I brood, I'm fun.

I affect all men
throughout their days
they look at me
in different ways.

To lovers
I should last forever
the imprisoned
think of me and shiver.

Some men buy me
to others a slave
I begin at the cradle
and end at the grave.

To others I'm lost
in their roses and wine
but forever I last
my name's...Old Man Time.

THE BATTLEFIELD WITHIN

Since the beginning of time,
all outward show of strength has been admired,
power and force,
blood and thunder,
plenty of noise,
that a destroys
whatever stands before it,
have been required,
reach the top,
and be the Boss,
for the King – A Country,
the Director – A Company,
the Soldier – A Victoria Cross.

But there are other men,
simple men,
men of the spirit,
quiet and austere,
sympathetical,
and full of care,
for the quality of life,
nature and beauty,
discipled,
with devotion to duty.

Their dress is humble,
their food is frugal,
behind a Monastery wall,
they fast and pray,
and early rise,
all day to till the soil.

In the face of the battle,
it seems that they'd scatter,
for their power,
seems shallow and small,
but in the end,
it's this truth they defend,
that the man who conquers himself,
is the greatest Warrior of all,
for the Monastery wall can be scaled,
but the Spirit of Man is forever,
within himself impaled.

THE NURSE

Shining bright,
guiding light,
caring day,
soothing night,
The Nurse

Running here,
dashing there,
"Fetch a bedpan,"
"Gie's a chair,"
The Nurse

Mothlike silhouettes,
dancing behind night screens,
comforting the valiant's pain,
or perhaps a fractured dream,
The Nurse

I'm beholding to them all,
for better or for worse
for I lost my hip,
to a Surgeon,
but I lost my heart,
to The Nurse.

Dedicated to all at Ward 28, Glasgow Royal Infirmary 1993.

THE SCAFFY

He's oot wi' his brush,
in the wind and the rain,
cleanin' the streets,
removin' the stain,
cleanin' the pavements,
cleanin' the stairs,
lookin' for culprits,
dropped everywhere,
empty fag packets,
beer cans that's dead,
chewin' gum wrappers,
papers that's read,
dirt and stoor,
and grit and grime,
every day o' the year,
every minute o' time,
but when he comes hame,
tae his Cooncil retreat,
his wife cries his name,
"Wullie...mind clean yer feet!"

Benny Lynch seen here with Boxing Promoter, George Dingley. Photograph by courtesy of the "Daily Record", Anderson Quay, Glasgow.

THE BOY FROM THE GORBALS

Benny Lynch, born in Glasgow,
to be a World Champ,
from a Gorbals slum,
wi' a smokey lum,
and walls that cried wi' damp.

He didnae eat Organic foods,
wear shoes wi' leather uppers,
he was clothed and fed,
in poverty's moods,
by the Brigait and greasy fish suppers.

He danced in puddles,
and dreeped fae dykes,
played hide and seek wi' rats,
and he skipped roon middens,
on warm summer nights,
and he clapped a thoosaun' cats.

But when he stood in a Boxing Ring
alone but never lonely,
he was majestic as a King,
was Benny, the one and only.

Suntanned 'Small Montana' from California,
was confident when he did meet him,
but he wasn't so keen,
after round thirteen,
when the Boy from the Gorbals did beat him.
He beat Jackie Brown,
and he beat Peter Kane,
beat dozens and dozens of others,
wi' a punch delivered,
wi' the speed of a train,
that sent them all hame to their Mothers.

Wi' a generous heart, and a giving hand,
he was welcomed all over the place,
but when wealth he had none,
and his credit was done,
poor Benny, had fallen from grace.

He was thirty three years,
when they laid him to rest,
in Lambhill, alone and forlorn,
he had fought wi' the greatest,
and beaten the best,
but he couldnae beat John Barleycorn.

Dedicated to a wee man with a big title.
"Flyweight Boxing Champion of the World."

BESPOKE JOCK

The English were made to rule
The Irish were made to rebel
The Welsh were made to sing
But,
The Scots were made to measure!

Mrs Catherine Forbes pictured in her Garngad home in 1963.
Photograph courtesy of the author.

MY WEE GRANNY

My Granny was the wisest wummin,
her common sense was no' sae common,
at ninety-one she filled a coffin in sweet repose,
and left a legacy of lovin' tae them and those.

Catherine, born in Bristol Town,
her parents had a gypsy flair,
defied the world's despondent frown,
wi' simple prayer,
and trusted in the Bountiful Lord
tae haundle care.

"A clear conscience is a soft pillow"
"Enough is as good as a feast"
"Goodness is its ain reward"
"And God put the man on the moon for breaking sticks on a Sunday"
She kept these sayings handy!

If she lived upon this day,
and saw the greed o' malcontents,
she'd shake her heid in sair dismay,
at foolish Kents,
a Government in disarray,
A' brains and nae sense!

Mrs Catherine Forbes
(The Author's Grandmother).

1st Battallion, 91st Division The Argyle & Sutherland Highlanders, Malta, 1912. Photograph: Courtesy of The Mitchell Library in Glasgow.

HI'ELAN LADDIE

I stand before thee,
as a Scottish Soldier,
life's conflicts I maun face,
afore I leave,
but the world shall know,
before the Battle's over,
we Scots shall never fill,
the coward's grave.

In fond memory of my Grandfather Archibald Forbes.
Who enlisted in 1898 aged 17 years. Registered No. 6772.
1st Battallion, 91st. Division, Argyle and Sutherland Highlanders.
Died 9th September 1962 aged 81 years.

TAE A GLESGA MOOSE

"There's a moose in the hoose,
it ran under the bed,
just like that!"
said my auld Granny.
Then I saw it mysel',
on the Old Lino Trail,
goin' tae the shops for its Mammy.

So doon went the trap,
for ower a week,
wi' cheese that was invitin',
every night he'd come oot,
an' gie a wee squeak,
then start his nocturnal bitin'.

But 'though he wis young,
and no' very smart,
and bein' sae very light,
he feenished the meal,
but eluded the trap,
night efter night, efter night.

Till wan night he wis caught,
between his nest and the bed,
separated fae hamely comforts,
he would sprint a bit here,
and dart a bit there,
mesmerisin' the fler wi' his efforts.

So wi' a shovel in hand,
at guard I did stand,
just behind the door,
then he made a great run,
but did foolishly staun,
in the middle o' the floor.
"Wham!"
Doon came the shovel,
wi' a helluva clatter,
and splatter...
an' because o' a' that,
a Glesga moose was buried flat.

Oh! wee innoculous, poetry friendly creature,
yer worrying me,
and scurrying me,
fair jeopardised yer future,
but, in spite o' a' that,
yur still a moose
but Man's a Rat!

TO A FRIEND

This truth shall guide my humble hand,
none shall profanely write Thy name,
and here upon my word shall stand,
the promise that a friend may claim,
and when in pensive mood inclined,
you turn your face and gently dee,
my name will praise with honour kind,
the pleasure of your company.

Joseph Jeffrey Esquire. – An Honourable Gentleman – Held in high esteem. Resident in Hyndland through good taste, born in the Calton through good fortune.

THE UNDERTAKER
(LE POMPES FUNÉBRES)

The Rid Biddy
(Bacchus by God)
is produced
in the lush vineyards of
La Belle Bourbonnais
and
ends up
in the belly
of a happy corpse
in Glesga Green.

Ye
dinnae tell us
that
your CV
(or should it be VP)
marked yer caird
as
a comparatively inexpensive
full bodied
cheeky wee swally
popular at Funerals so ye dinnae

Ah mean
La Belle Bourbonnais
it even sounds thrapple friendly
and Glesga Green
on a perishin' day in the middle o' March
nae comparison Jaques
nae comparison.

ALONE NO MORE

Loneliness
you purged my soul
Loneliness
my oldest friend.

Loneliness
your time is tholed
for in you
I thought of many things.

And in the end
found God
and I rejoice
in looking back.

How well you have
done your chore
as I kneel
to pray this night
in peace,
alone no more.

LET THE PUNISHMENT FIT THE COAT

"Your Honour Sir
I was drinking heavily
I was out of my mind
I didn't mean to cause such strife."

"Young man, then I'll spare you the Jailor
sanity wears many coats
so find a good Tailor
and enjoy life."

"Your Honour Sir
your judgement is fair
but what kind of coat
could a bloke like me wear
to recompense?"

"Young man, wear the one you were born with
it suited you well
then you had elegance
then you were a swell
...wear innocence."

THE MAN IN MY MIRROR

Sometimes he scribes
the Poet's pen
but now and then
then mair again
He's just a drunk exhibit.

The poetic Wan
is a Gentleman
but until he's free
fae Auld Hornie's glee
the Demons aye will visit!

THE CHRISTMAS DIPLOMAT

The local butcher and his staff had worked from early morn until late on Christmas Eve, providing the local populace with all their Christmas fare.

Just as he was about to close the shop, in walked a very old woman in a shawl.

"Could ye gie me a chicken for ma Christmas dinner?" she asked him hopefully.

The butcher on looking around, knew his trays were empty but, not wanting to disappoint the old woman at Christmas, replied, "Haud oan, I'll check ma fridge."

In the fridge he found one solitary chicken hanging on a hook, the last in the shop.

"Thank the Lord," muttered the butcher in a rare moment of Presbyterian abandon.

Weighing it in front of the old woman as he said, "Seeing it's Christmas you can have it for five shillings."

She hesitated for a moment, "Dae ye no' hiv a bigger wan?" she asked.

Not only a Master Butcher was Bill, but also a Master Diplomat.

"Jist a minute, I'll hae another wee look," said he, as he made his way back to the fridge.

Twenty seconds later he emerged, carrying the same chicken which he proceeded to put on the scales.

"You're in luck Missus, this wan's heavier, it'll be seven and six pence."

The old woman looked at him with a smile on her face and said,

"Guid, wrap the two o' them up, ah'll hiv them baith."

47

YESTERDAY

"Wan, two, three a leerie,
I'll lend ye ma gird, if ye lend me yer peerie."
Playing Blind Man's Bluff tae keep thursel' cheery,
and skipping ropes, never made them weary,
Glesga's Olympic Weans!

Hunch, cuddy, hunch, an' kick the can,
tig yer het, if ye never ran,
wee heiders and rounders, and catch-me-if-ye-can,
but, ye never played peever...if ye wur a man!
Laughter wis in thur banes!

Beds chalked on pavements, goal posts on the wa',
wi' three holes in the groon fur bools big and sma',
and twenty-a-side, wi' a tanner ba',
then a big jeely piece thrown doon by yer Maw,
Will Ye No' Come Back Again!